I Spy with all 5 Eyes...

Pollinator Coloring & Activity Book

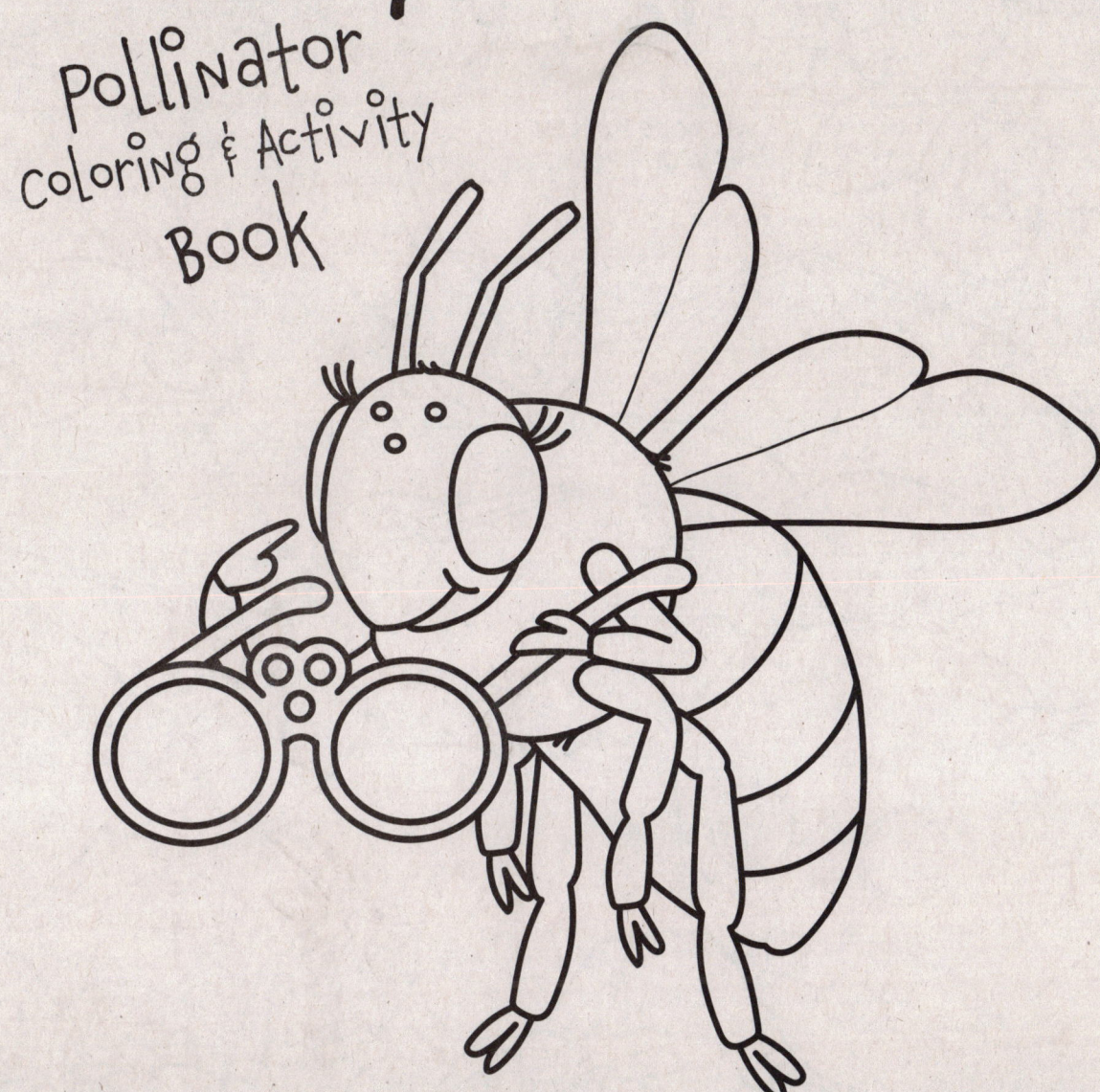

Written by Charlotte Hubbard and Kimi Baker
www.hubbardhive.com and www.livingthatloghomelife.com
Artwork by Carolyn Fink, www.carolynfink.com

Copyright ©2024 by Charlotte Hubbard, Publisher
11046 Higley Circle West; Schoolcraft, MI. 49087
All Rights Reserved Worldwide

This is Blossom. She is hiding on **16 pages** in this book. Can you find her?

I Spy with all 5 Eyes...

Pollination
We pollinators help plants make fruit and vegetables.

WE MOVE POLLEN FROM ONE PLANT ...

...TO ANOTHER PLANT OF THE SAME TYPE.

2

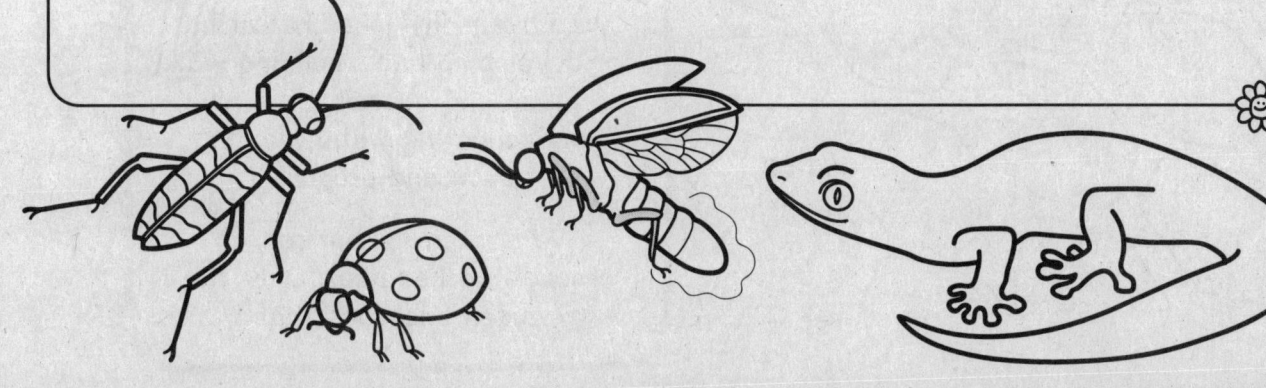

pollinators!

word search

```
B V B N H D T M M O N A R C H Z Z L
E Z U S Q U G S O Y M L P W I N D C
E J T F A V M M Y T Y J A O F N B N
T C T F Q S S M K D H X Q D L U A Q
L E E O H V F F I R E F L Y Y L M E
E H R N P O L L I N A T I O N B E W
O G F E P H Y L O W G K B D M B U N
K E L C U V K Y B W U B V I U E J G
C C Y T B X G C O P E D I W R P G S
Q K S A E A W A S P U R J R W D J E
M O K R F D T H O R N E T E D W A A
W L I Z A R D Y L E M U R B E P D N
```

CAN YOU FIND THESE WORDS?

BAT	BUTTERFLY	GECKO	LEMUR	NECTAR	WASP
BEE	FIREFLY	HORNET	LIZARD	POLLEN	WIND
BEETLE	FLY	HUMMINGBIRD	MONARCH	POLLINATION	
BIRD	FLOWER	LADYBUG	MOTH		

I Spy with all 5 Eyes...

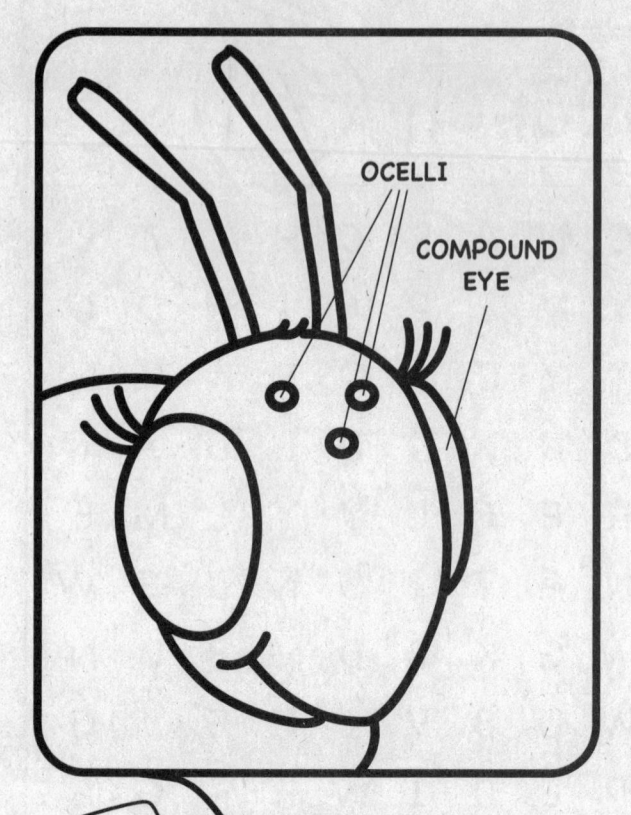

OCELLI

COMPOUND EYE

We have five eyes, but it might be hard to see them at first.

We also have four wings, but it looks like two. Our wings beat over **200** times per second, that's why we buzz.

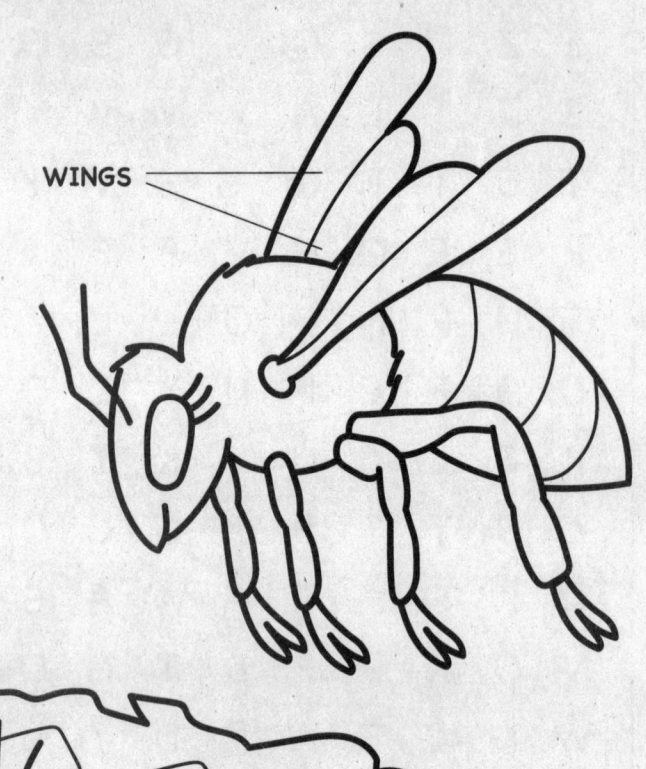

WINGS

Worker Bees
We have many jobs like caring for developing bees, building wax, cleaning and guarding the hive, and collecting water, nectar, pollen and propolis.

We are female, but cannot produce worker bees. Only the queen bee does that.

honey bees!

Queen Bee
I am usually the only queen in my hive. During the active season, I lay over 1,000 eggs daily!

THE QUEEN HAS A LONGER ABDOMEN THAN THE WORKERS.

Drone Bee
Drones are the male bees in the hive.

ONE WAY DRONES STAND OUT IS THEIR VERY LARGE EYES.

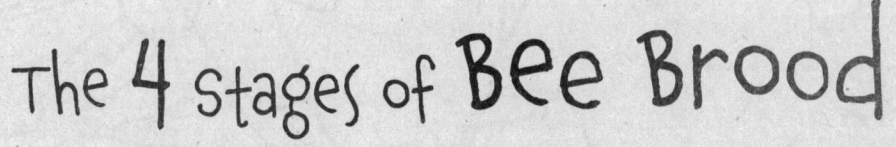

The 4 stages of Bee Brood

1. EGG
2. LARVA
3. PUPA
4. ADULT

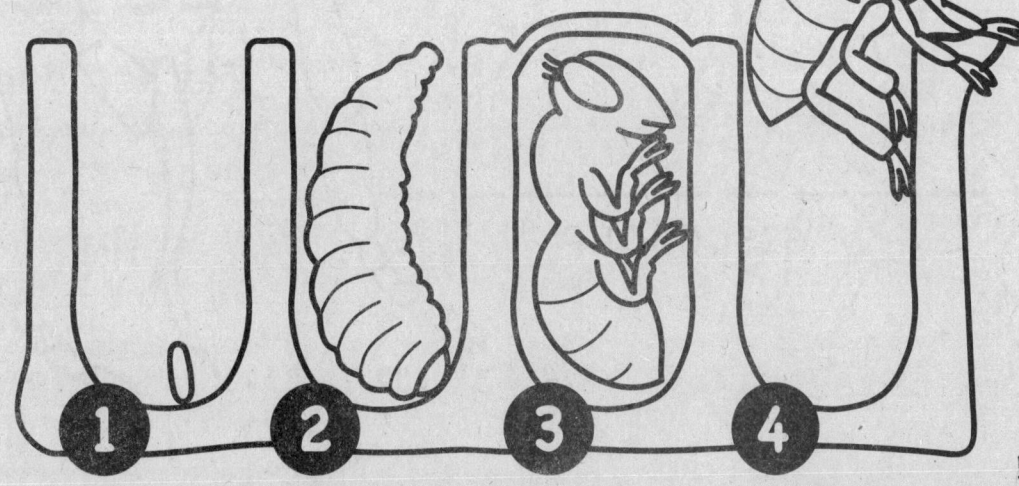

I Spy with all 5 Eyes...

Unscramble these letters to make bee body part words. Draw a line to connect each word to the body part.

_ _ _ _ _ _
XTHAOR

_ _ _ _
YESE
(5 of them!)

_ _ _ _
EDAH

_ _ _ _ _ _ _
NENANTA

_ _ _ _ _ _ _ _ _
SISCOBORP

parts of a bee!

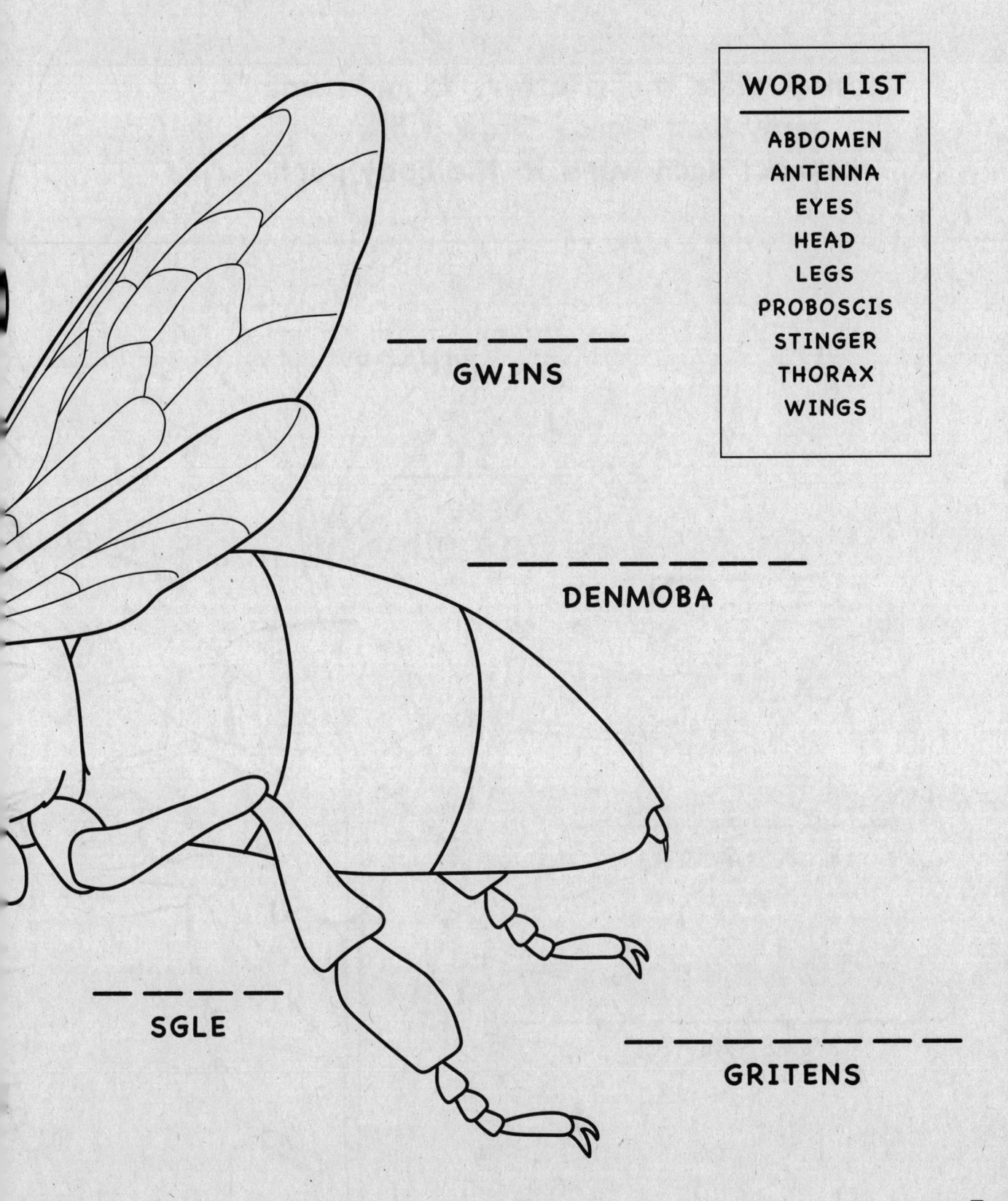

WORD LIST
- ABDOMEN
- ANTENNA
- EYES
- HEAD
- LEGS
- PROBOSCIS
- STINGER
- THORAX
- WINGS

_ _ _ _ _
GWINS

_ _ _ _ _ _ _
DENMOBA

_ _ _ _
SGLE

_ _ _ _ _ _ _
GRITENS

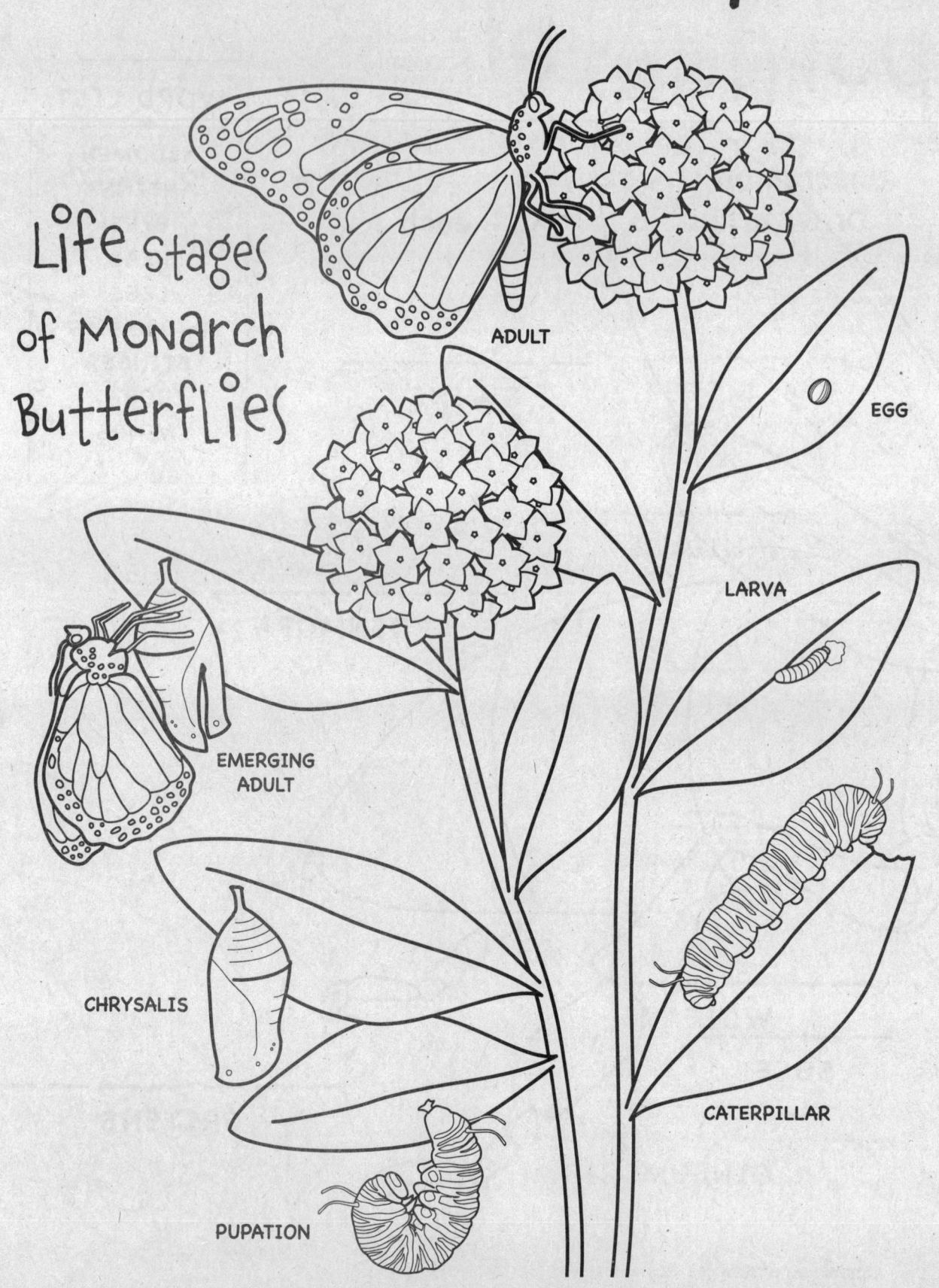

I Spy with all 5 eyes...

Life stages of Monarch Butterflies

ADULT

EGG

LARVA

EMERGING ADULT

CHRYSALIS

CATERPILLAR

PUPATION

more friends who help pollinate!

Unscramble these letters to make pollinator words. Draw a line to connect each word to its picture.

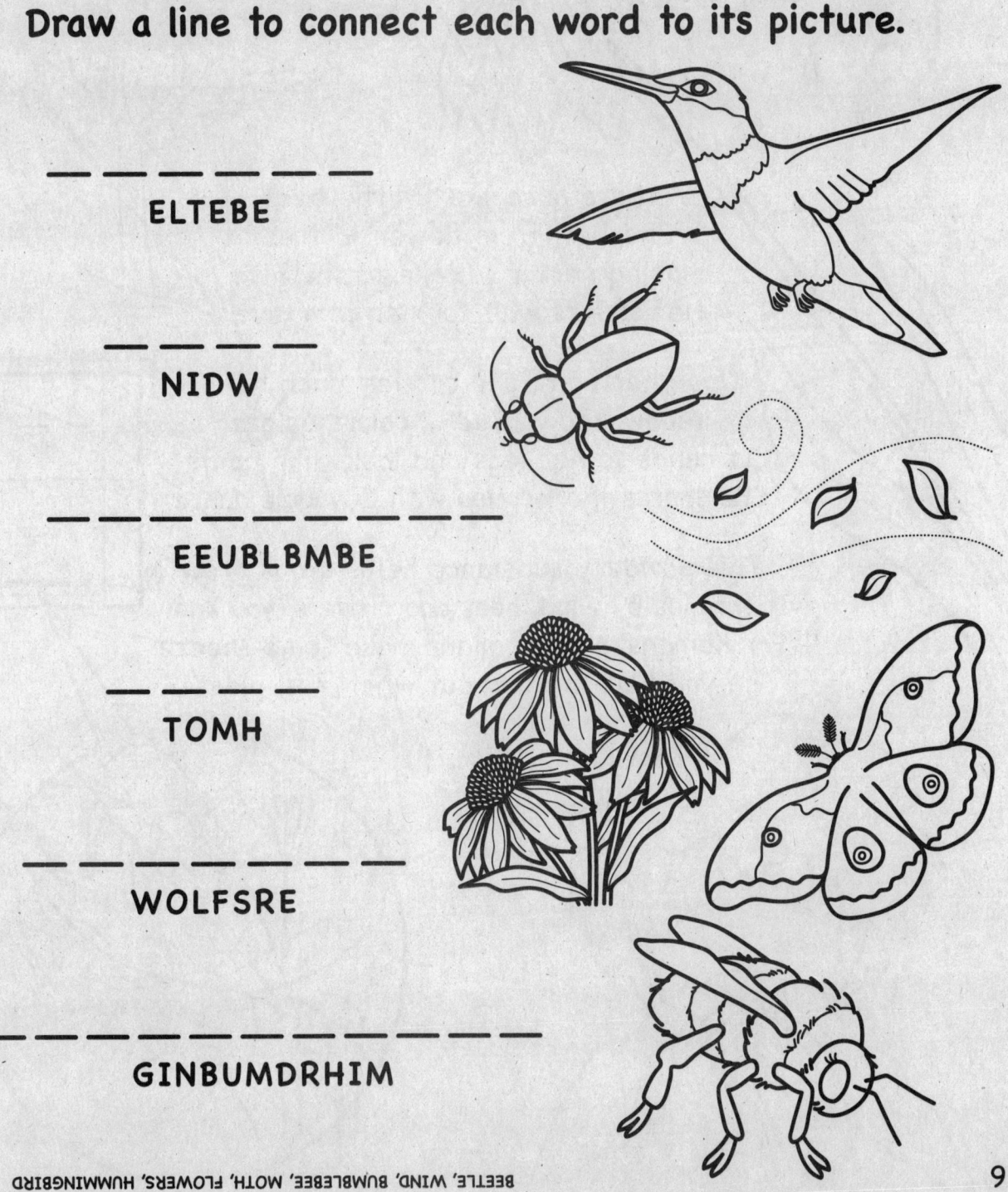

_ _ _ _ _ _
ELTEBE

_ _ _ _
NIDW

_ _ _ _ _ _ _ _ _
EEUBLBMBE

_ _ _ _
TOMH

_ _ _ _ _ _ _
WOLFSRE

_ _ _ _ _ _ _ _ _ _
GINBUMDRHIM

BEETLE, WIND, BUMBLEBEE, MOTH, FLOWERS, HUMMINGBIRD

I Spy with all 5 Eyes...

There once was a little bee
She flew from flower to tree
Sipping nectar to take to the hive
Her sisters wait for her to arrive

Upon her body, she carries much more
Yellow, brown, red ... colors galore
It clings to her legs and looks like pants
She shares the location with a waggle dance

This powdery substance helps crops grow
It spreads by wind, bees and critters, you know
For humans, well, it might make some sneeze
Can you help me find out what it is, please?

10

fun with pollination!

This powdery substance comes in so many colors!

Color the cells by number to reveal the answer to the poem on the previous page.

Then write the answer into the blanks by the bee on this page.

1 YELLOW
2 LT. GREEN
3 DARK GREEN
4 BLUE
5 RED
6 BLACK
7 GRAY
8 ORANGE
9 LT. BROWN
10 PURPLE

WHEN A WORKER BEE STUFFS

_ _ _ _ _ _ _

INTO SPECIAL POCKETS ON HER HIND LEGS, SOME BEEKEEPERS SAY SHE'S WEARING

_ _ _ _ _ _ _ PANTS.

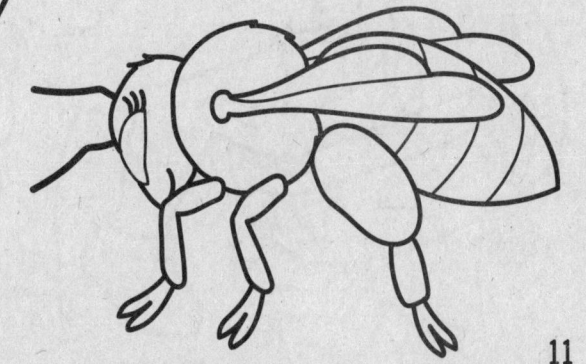

I Spy with all 5 eyes...

Can you find at least 15 things that start with B?

things that start with B!

Add and write the answers in the hexagons. Connect the answers to the right number of pollinators.

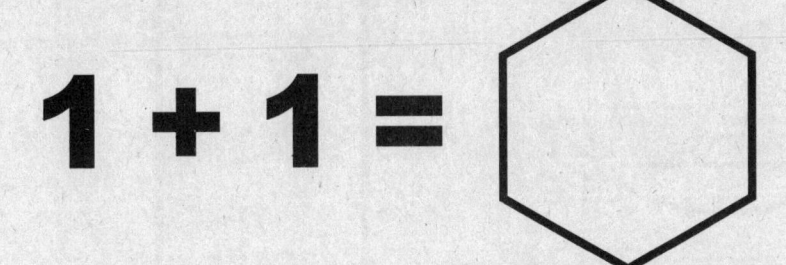

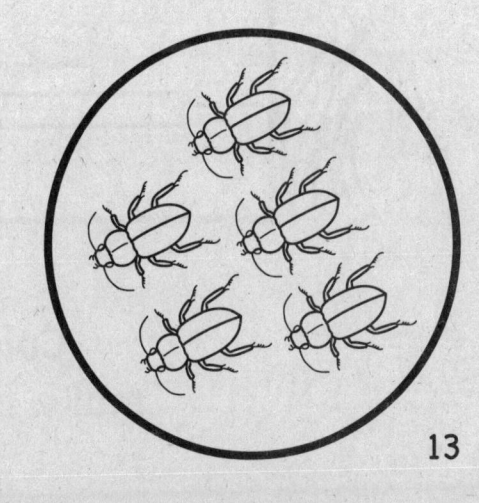

2 + 1 =

1 + 1 =

3 + 2 =

ANSWERS: 3, 2, 5

13

I Spy with all 5 Eyes...

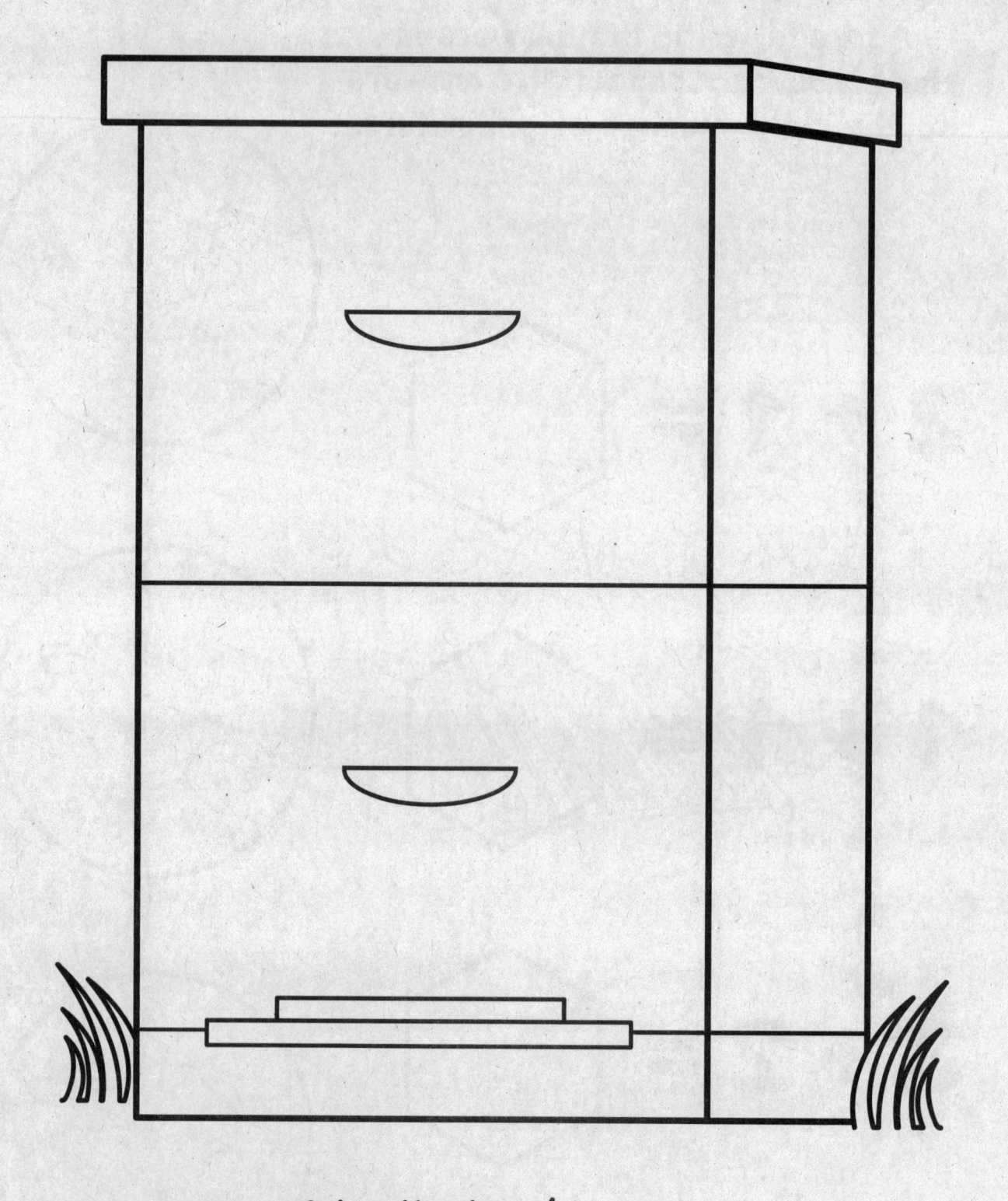

Color the bees' home —
make it fun for you and them.

a great place for honey bees to live!

WE BUILD WAX CELLS — HONEYCOMB!
IT HOLDS HONEY, POLLEN, AND BABY BEES.

I Spy with all 5 eyes...

We collect nectar and turn it into yummy honey.

Flowers make **NECTAR**.

We sip it up with a special tongue called a **PROBOSCIS**.

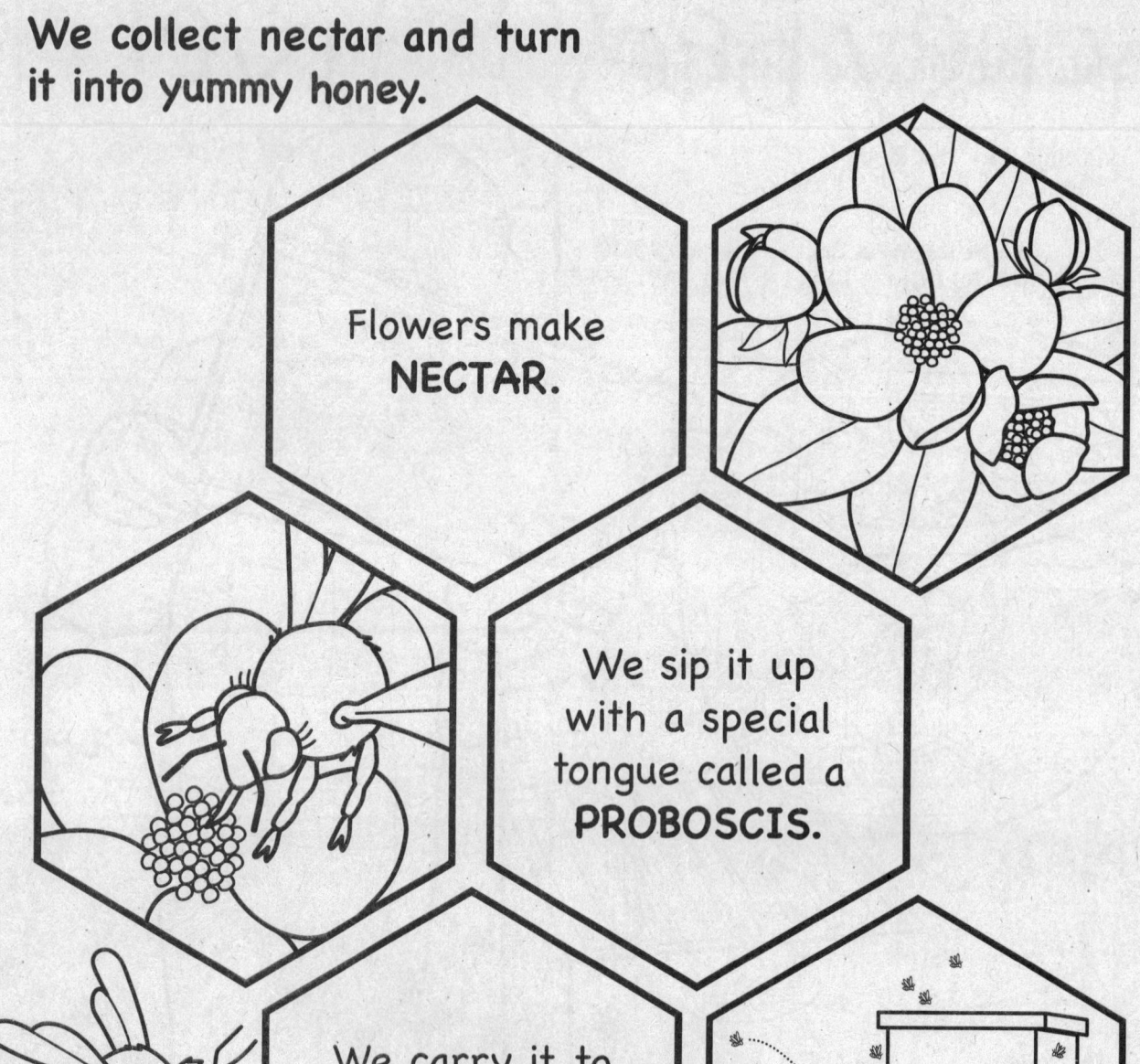

We carry it to our hive in a **SPECIAL STOMACH**.

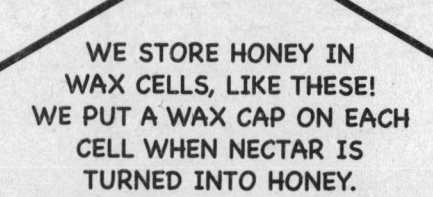

WE FLY ABOUT 55,000 MILES TO COLLECT ENOUGH NECTAR TO MAKE A POUND OF HONEY!

WE STORE HONEY IN WAX CELLS, LIKE THESE! WE PUT A WAX CAP ON EACH CELL WHEN NECTAR IS TURNED INTO HONEY.

what we ♡ to eat!

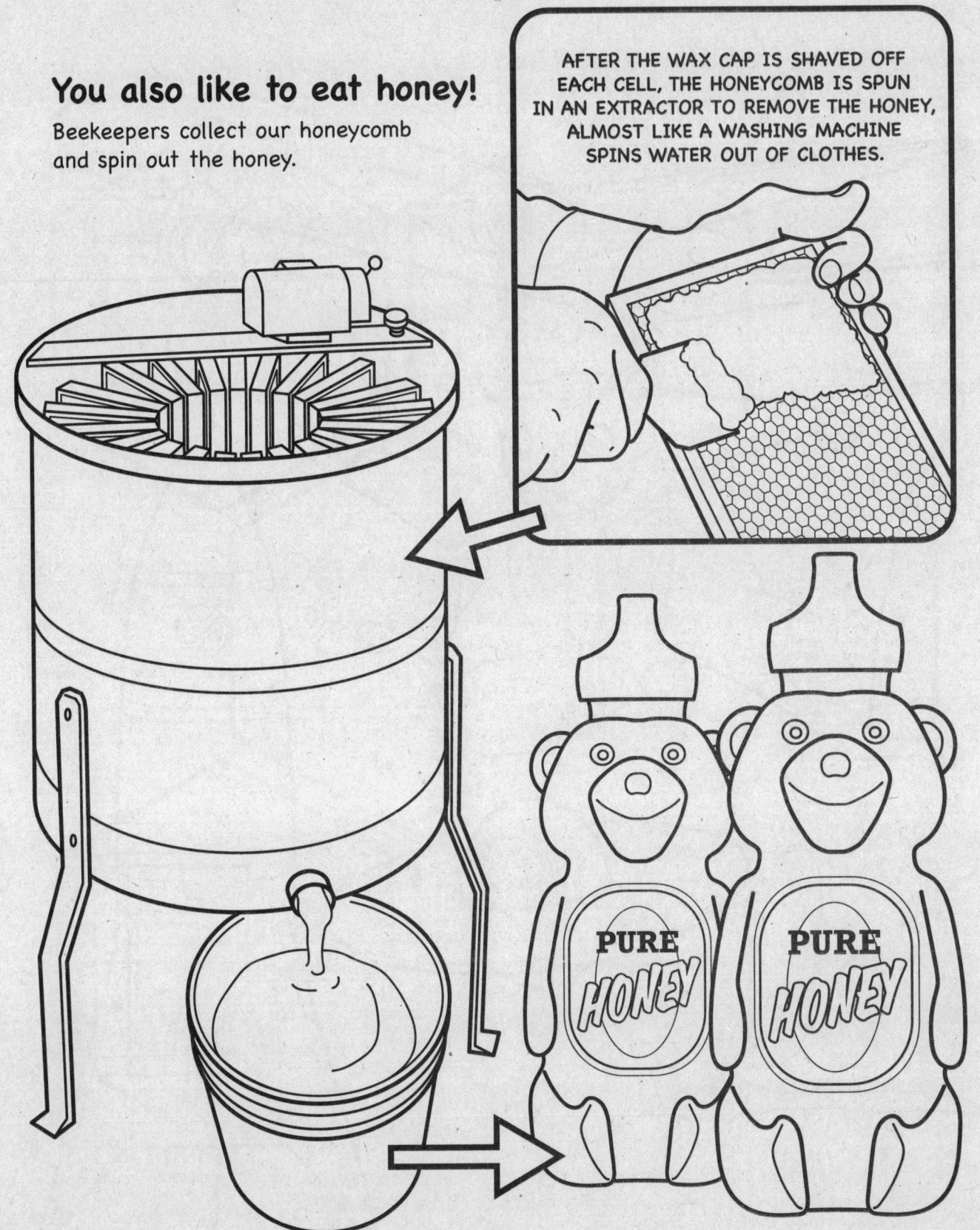

You also like to eat honey!
Beekeepers collect our honeycomb and spin out the honey.

AFTER THE WAX CAP IS SHAVED OFF EACH CELL, THE HONEYCOMB IS SPUN IN AN EXTRACTOR TO REMOVE THE HONEY, ALMOST LIKE A WASHING MACHINE SPINS WATER OUT OF CLOTHES.

PURE HONEY

PURE HONEY

17

I Spy with all 5 eyes...

other things that fly!

I Spy with all 5 eyes...

Circle the differences in these pictures.

differences in these pictures!

See answers on page 40.

I Spy with all 5 Eyes...

In the summer, one hive of bees uses about 2 gallons of water per week.

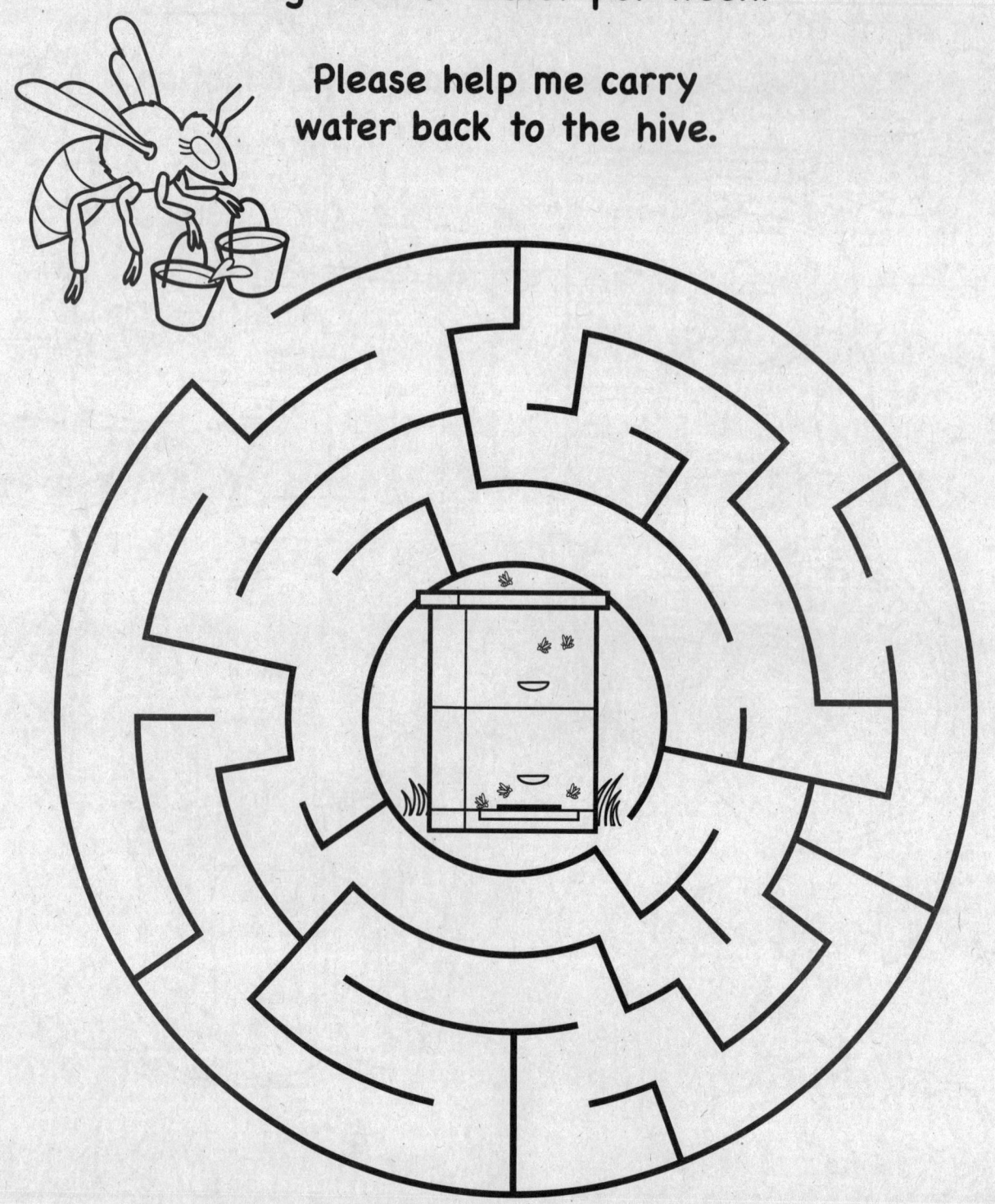

Please help me carry water back to the hive.

busy bees!

Honey bees give directions to things like water and flowers with a "waggle dance."

We move our bodies in a particular motion.
Can you do it, too?

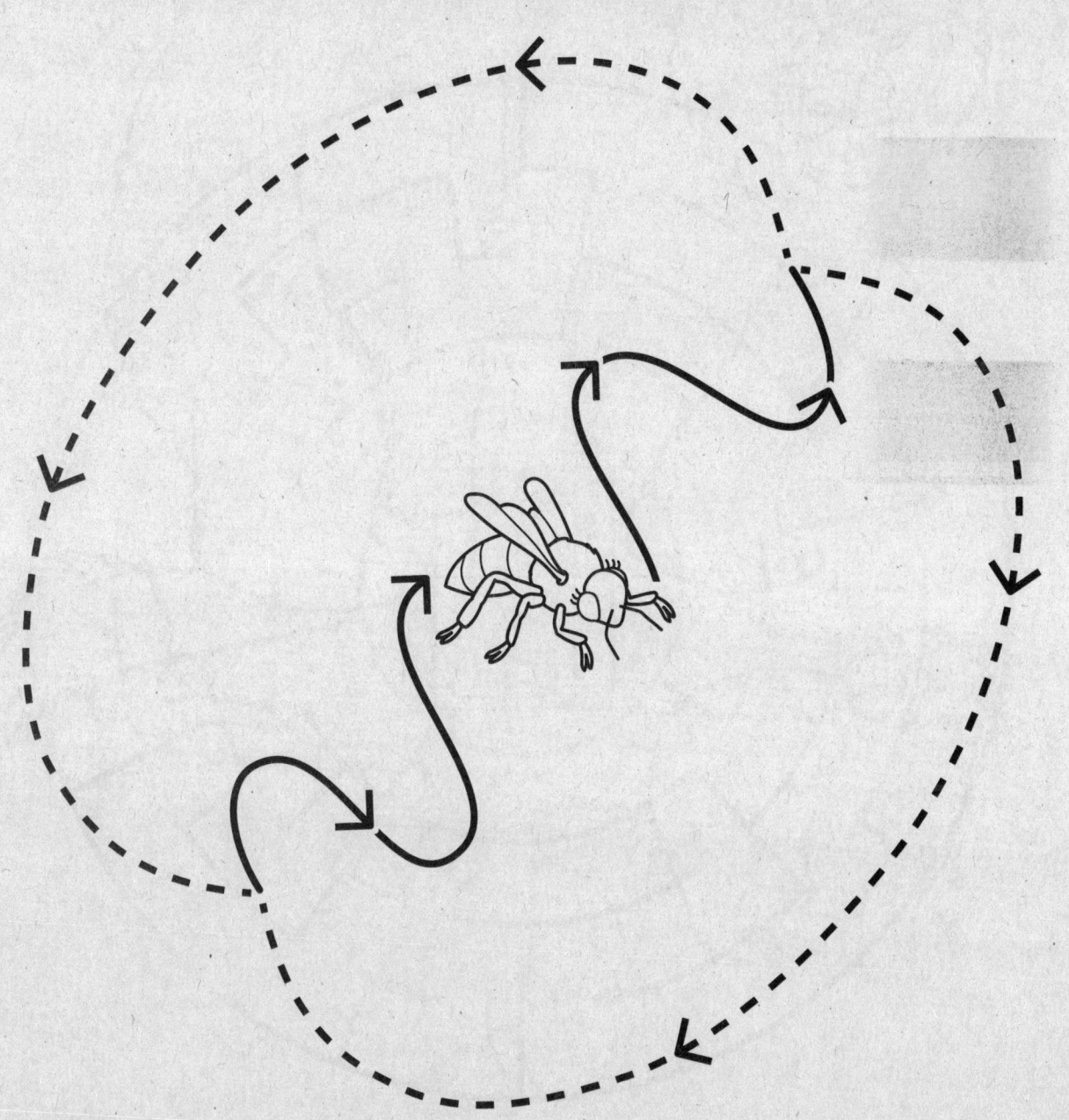

I Spy with all 5 eyes...

Some wild animals tear open hives to eat yummy food.

24

danger!

Watch your step!
Honey bees sting when they feel threatened.
Even if you don't mean to step on one, she will sting
to protect herself and the hive.

I Spy with all 5 Eyes...

A bug that bugs us is the Varroa mite.
They are found in bee colonies throughout the world.

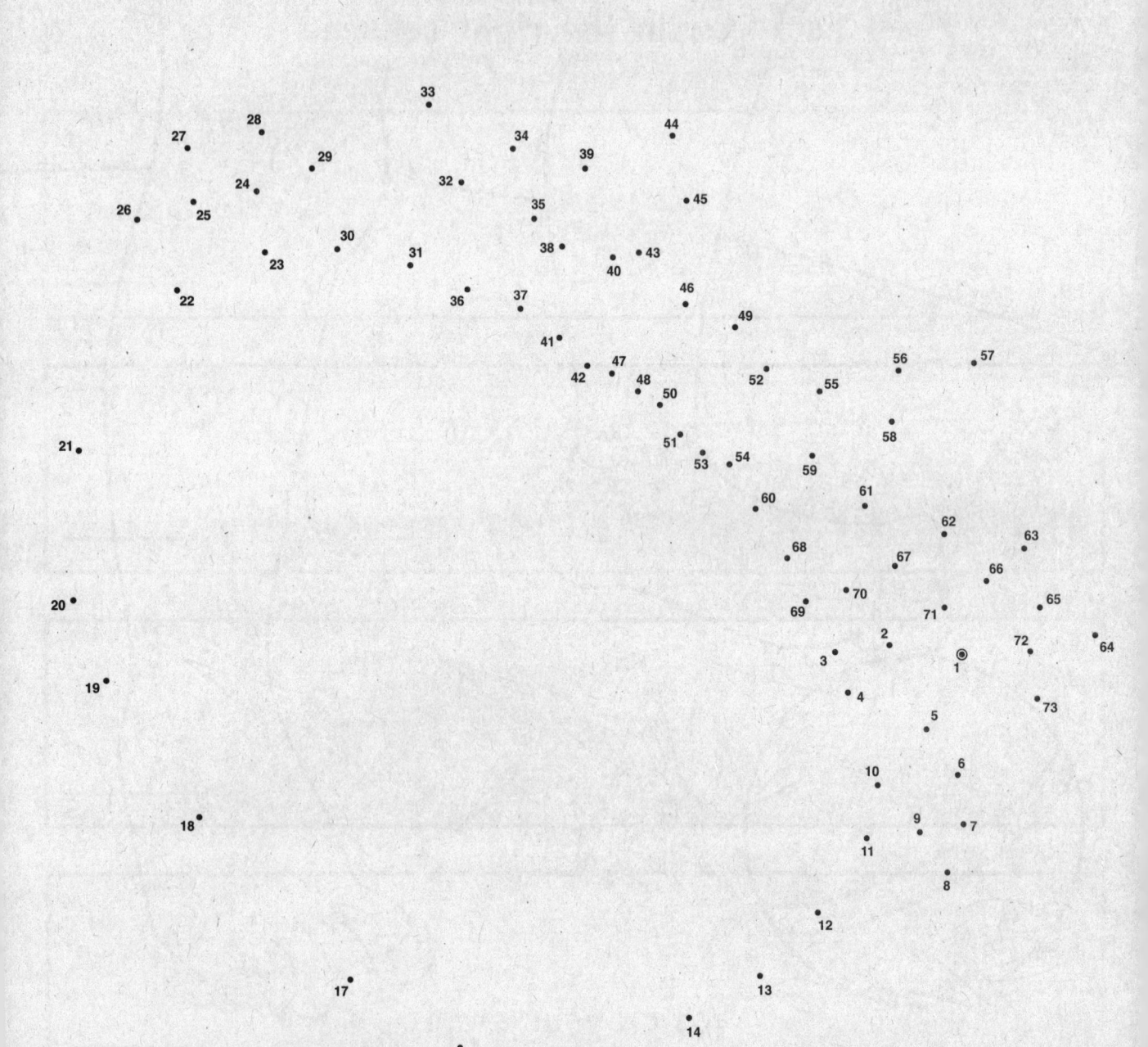

26

things that don't belong!

Some of these things are not like the others. Circle the item in each row that doesn't belong. Then, write how many pollinators are in each row in the right column.

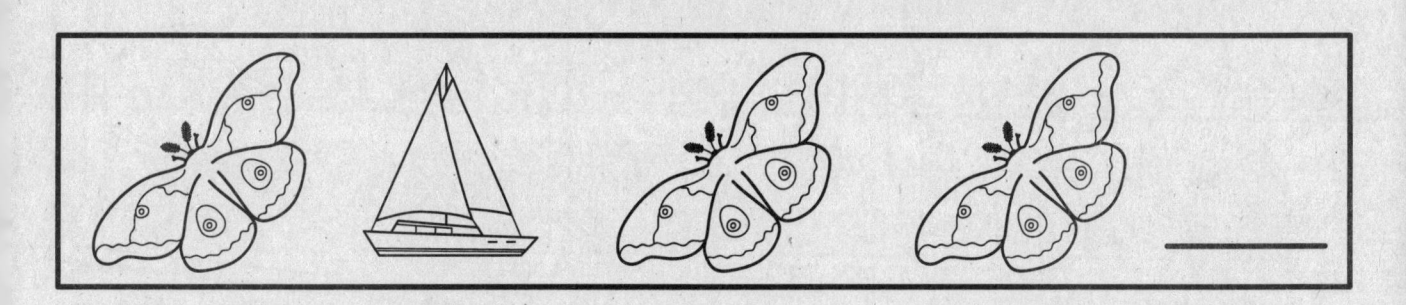

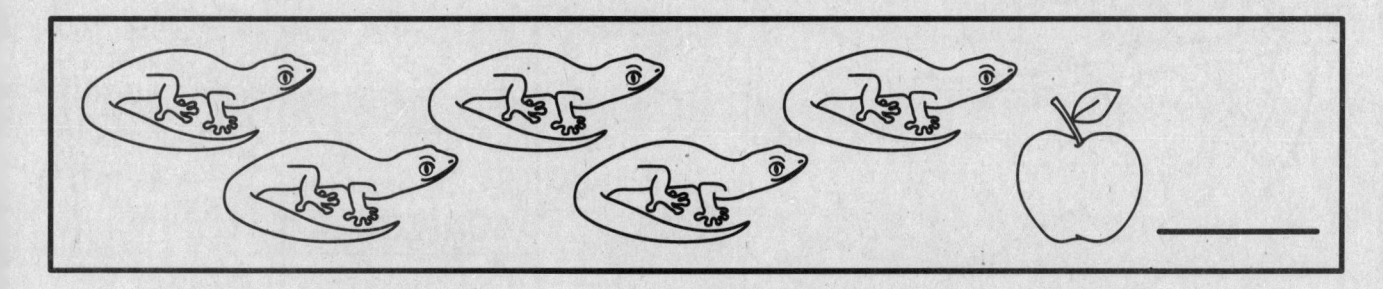

ANSWERS: 3, 4, 3, 5

I Spy with all 5 eyes...

Crabapple Cherry Basswood

BEE BALM SEEDS

SUNFLOWER SEEDS

ALYSSUM SEEDS

28

things you can do to help pollinators!

HUMMINGBIRDS BEAT THEIR WINGS MORE THAN 4,000 TIMES PER MINUTE AND CAN EVEN FLY BACKWARDS!

Please help this hummingbird find the feeder.

I Spy with all 5 Eyes...

1 in 3 bites of food requires a pollinator.

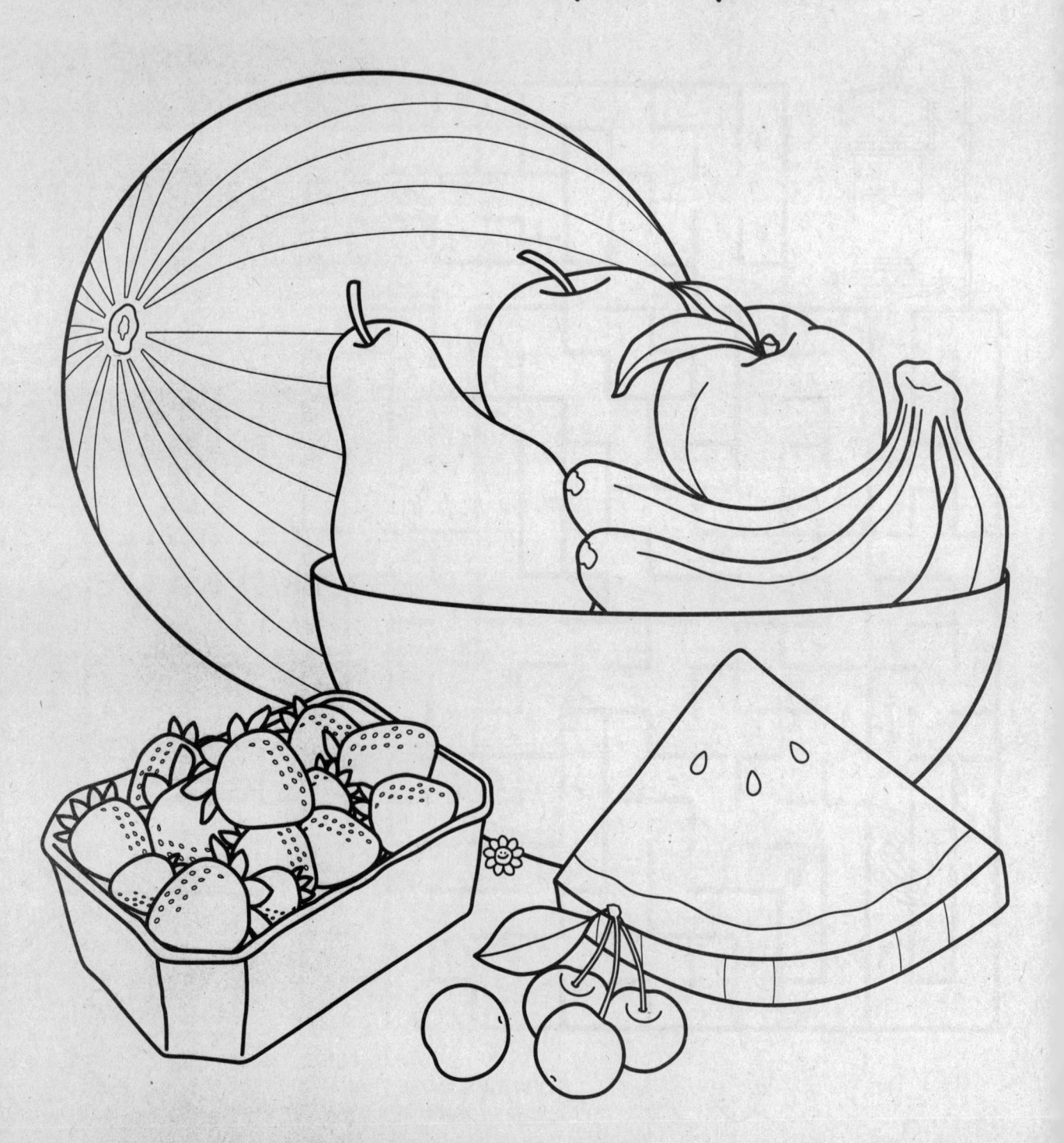

foods that need pollinators!

What are the answers to these equations?

🍓 + 🍎 = _____

🍒 + 🍓 + 🎃 = _____

🍎 + 🎃 + 🎃 = _____

🍒 + 🥜 + 🍎 = _____

🥜 + 🎃 + 🍓 = _____

USE THE KEY BELOW TO SOLVE

1: strawberry 2: almond 3: pumpkin 4: apple 5: cherries

ANSWERS: 5, 9, 10, 11, 6

I Spy with all 5 Eyes...

Connect the dots to reveal a type of fruit and to find out who pollinates it.

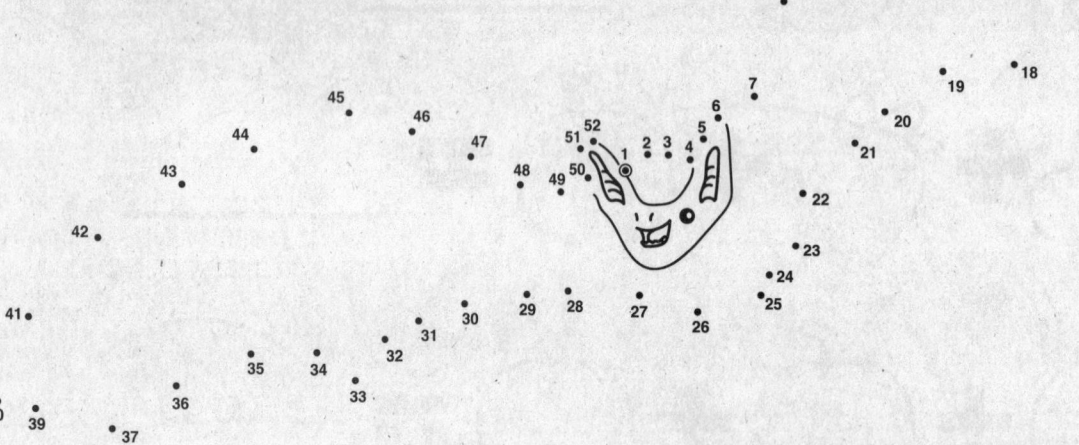

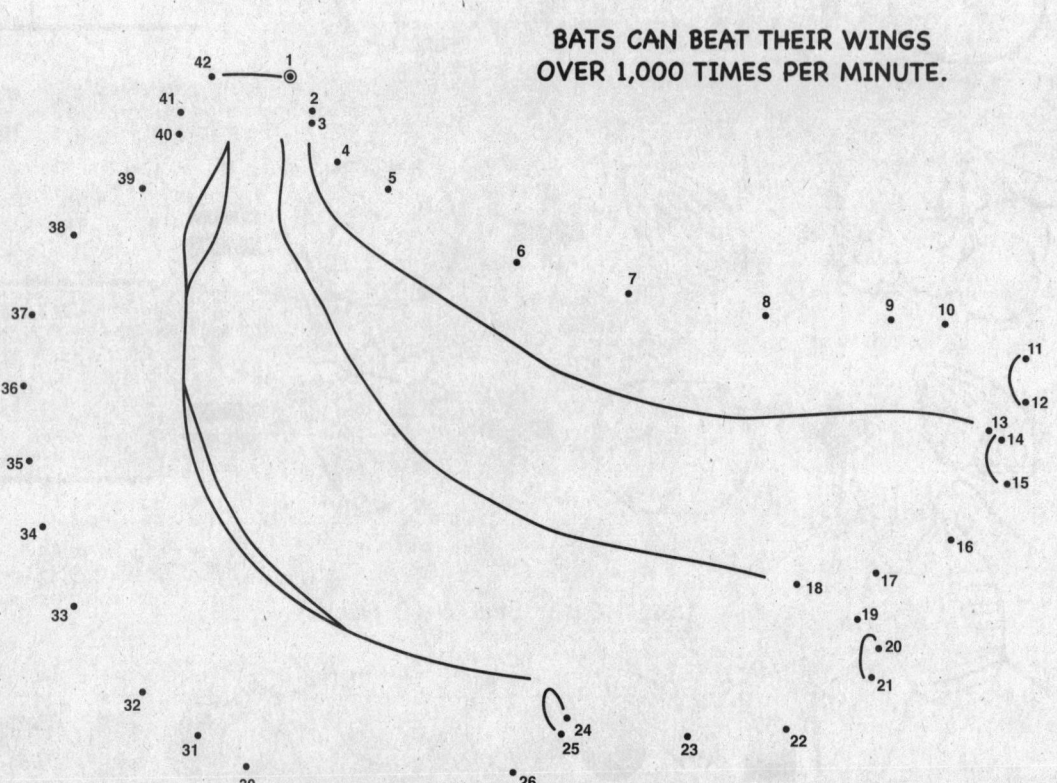

BATS CAN BEAT THEIR WINGS OVER 1,000 TIMES PER MINUTE.

32

WILD BANANAS ARE POLLINATED BY THE FRUIT BAT.

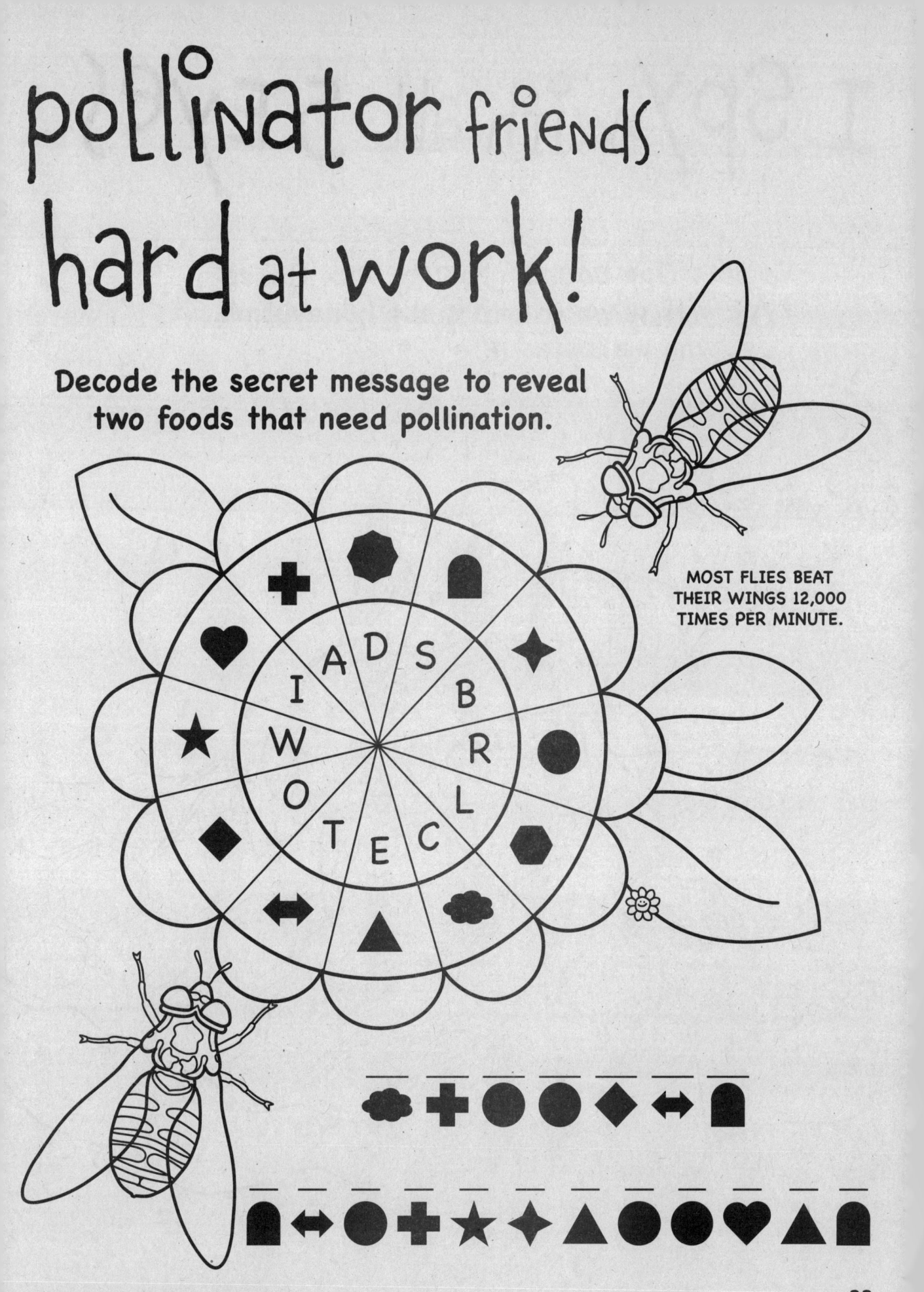

pollinator friends hard at work!

Decode the secret message to reveal two foods that need pollination.

MOST FLIES BEAT THEIR WINGS 12,000 TIMES PER MINUTE.

ANSWERS: CARROTS, STRAWBERRIES

I Spy with all 5 eyes...

Our bodies produce wax flakes that we use to make honeycomb.

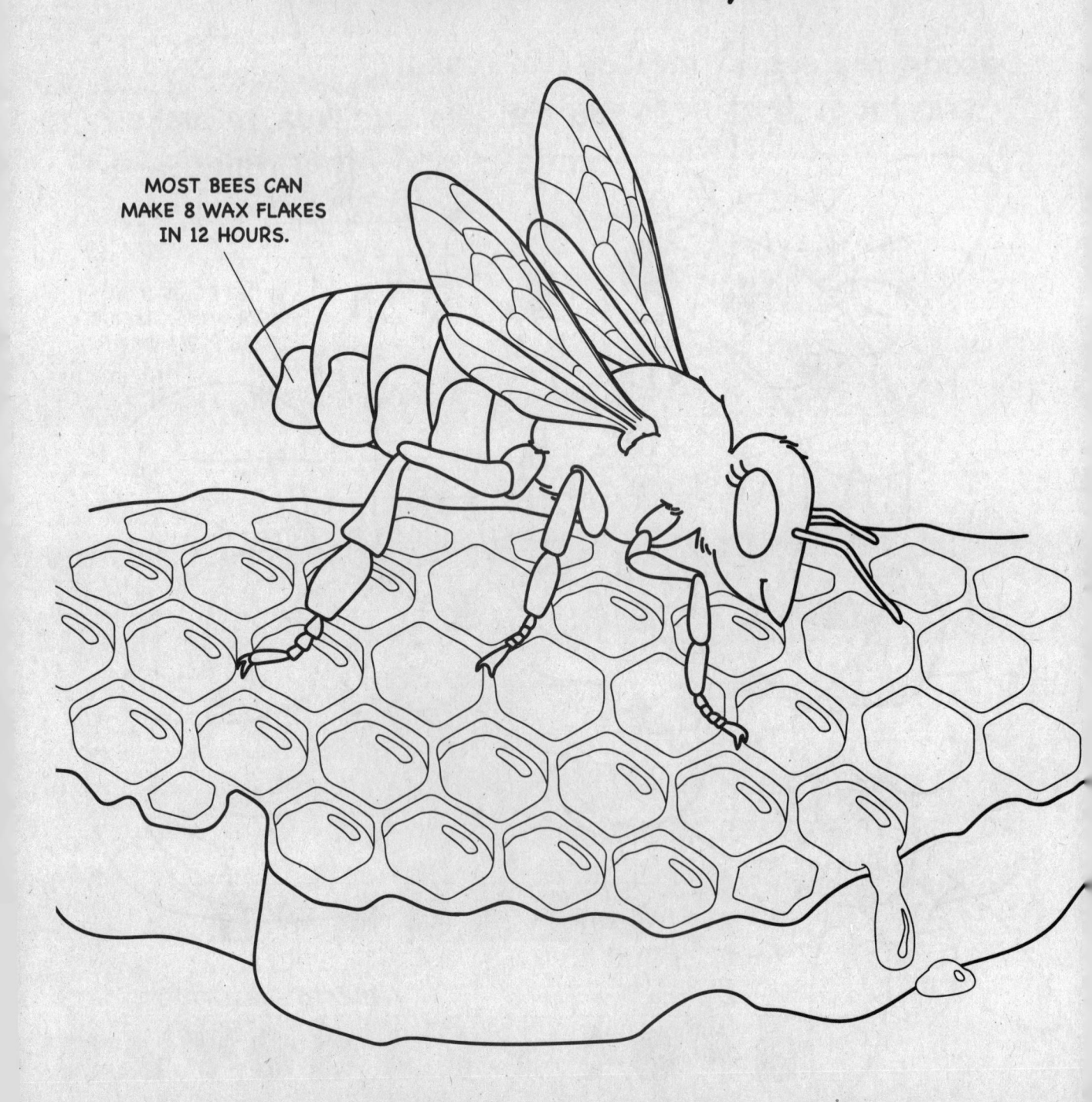

MOST BEES CAN MAKE 8 WAX FLAKES IN 12 HOURS.

honey bees producing wax!

You can use our wax to make candles and other things.

THIS CANDLE USES ABOUT
70,000 WAX FLAKES.

THIS CANDLE USES ABOUT
21,000 WAX FLAKES.

I Spy with all 5 eyes...

other items we help you make!

PURE HONEY

I Spy with all 5 EYES...

people learning about pollinators!

What kind of pollinator would you like to be?
Draw a picture of your favorite pollinator.

I Spy with all 5 Eyes... great resources!

List of Beekeeping Resources
https://pastatebeekeepers.org/education

Kid and Parent Bee Activities
https://xerces.org/education

Bee Activities and Articles for Kids
https://www.beeculture.com/category/bee-life/kids/

Polymer Clay Bee Activity and Bee Info
https://climatekids.nasa.gov/bees/

Kid Activity Posters
https://honey.com/bees-sustainability/educational-materials

Printable Kid Puzzles and Kid Fact Sheets
https://www.buzzaboutbees.net/bee-themed-educational-resources.html

Printable Kid Puzzles
https://michiganbees.org/bee-curious-worksheets

Answers for pages 20-21:

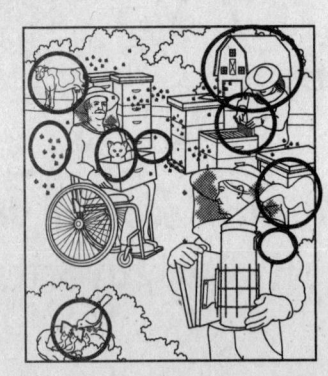

Blossom may be found on pages 3, 4, 8, 10, 12, 15, 18, 21, 23, 24, 29, 30, 33, 36, 37, 39.